AND I QUOTE...

Authentic thoughts of Inspiration

By

Mario L Martin

Table of Contents

Introduction

Congratulations! You have purchased a series of archived quotes and thoughts from my mind and/or mouth that have helped many before you. I hope they will also help give you inspiration, motivation, or reevaluation of some of your daily thoughts, and routine.

As a certified Life Coach, spiritual counselor, and Pastor I run across many people from day to day. I am frequently asked for my point of view and perspective on subjects that range from religion, politics, and relationships. Often, I discover that people find it easier to simply relax and slip off into what I call a dead zone. Aimlessly wandering through life. Aimlessly attending church, clubs, meetings, and seminars with no real drive, motivation, or direction. Many have expressed how they are discouraged because it seems that the odds are against them. Many have surrendered to the self-limiting beliefs that life will get no better. I disagree. I regularly use social media as a platform to uplift, encourage, and inspire people to meet their individual appointment with their purpose. The contents of this book are a compilation of quotes posted and/or given over a period that seem to have helped, encouraged, and/or inspired many others.

I pray that my unique sense of humor, my compassion for people, and strong desire to encourage will be of aid to you on your personal journey. Whether you're a writer, an artist, a minister, or simply someone who wants to grow as a person, I believe you will find many of these quotes usable. Now, check out the table of contents and quickly grab a random quote!

What I said… "About God"

This is the section of the book that gives tribute to leading influence in my life.

Having a relationship with the God of my salvation makes every day encouraging. It reminds me that there is no reason to ever give up when I've got God on my side.

How do you describe God? What words can you use to describe who and what he is in your heart? The Bible does this literarily. Here are a few quotes to get you started expressing your own experiences.

Christians should appreciate this part of the book. Others, well…Not so much.

What I said... "About God"

Authentic thoughts of Inspiration

- "His Joy reaches beyond the surface! It penetrates past the emotional part of me and reaches the sour, dark parts of my heart... healing my hurt, mending the brokenness, lifting what has sunken, and strengthening my weakness! It comforts the isolated and overshadows every memory of failure...Thank you God for JOY...DOWN DEEP IN MY SOUL!"   *- M L MARTIN*

- "There is one real source of Spiritual Power. For everything that God has provided us to be able to do, Satan has a counterfeit. Idolatry, witchcraft, necromancy, psychic hotline, illicit-mind altering drugs, "magic" (especially black magic and sorcery such as casting spells) are all birthed out of a spirit of rebellion... it makes man/woman more vulnerable to spiritual attacks, spiritual oppression, and spiritual possession... These are Satan's way of saying to us "if you eat of the fruit, you will not surely die... you will be like God" in the way he tricked Eve. This characteristic of Satan is the whole reason Hell exists in the first place. He thought to be exalted to an equal or superior level than God. And this is the trick he continually uses to lure mankind to Hell with him, as to say, "I don't need God, I am everything I need". Walk away from it all and give your life to Jesus. Trust in him and his Power only." - *M L MARTIN*

- God is Credible, because he's got such a consistent record of incredibility.
  - *M L MARTIN*

- Go back to ancestors and I'm going back further…Before there were ancestors there was God. Gen. 1:1, John 1:1 – *M L MARTIN*

- You will draw more people telling them what "God IS like" than telling them what "God "Doesn't" like"… -*M L MARTIN*

- Draw Nearer to God and watch him make your greatest fear, your favorite joke.
  - *M L MARTIN*

- "If you want God to Grow it, you'll first need to Sow it" – *M L MARTIN*

- "How any of you can ever let someone change your mind about Jesus... I DON'T KNOW???? I don't care what THEY read, I don't care what THEY wrote...I know what I felt. I know what I experienced. I saw it... eyes opened, bones restored, miracles happened... demons were cast out... I was there... I tried it... I called upon the name of the Lord and I'm a WITNESS... there is still... INDEED POWER in the Name JESUS. Spoken just like that. Even Pronounced just like that."   - *M L MARTIN*

- **Proverbs 27:5 KJV**

5 Open rebuke is better than secret love.

If your definition of love is allowing ppl to do whatever they want to do... You are a misrepresentation of Love.

1. *•Spare not the rod, - Parents to children*

2. *•God chastens whom he loves. - God to us*

3. *•If you love me, keep my commandments... -You to Jesus.*

Me to you:

True love should produce a positive, progressive change, and not passive, pacifying, comfort.

-M L MARTIN

Chapter Summary/Key Takeaways

It is important to remember that no one person has any patent on how God can be described. If we are all different, then we will all have different opinions, experiences, and understanding. Yet, there is a bottom line; No one can fully define your relationship with God. Or determine what you think about God. What is he to you?

What we think about God ultimately shapes our behavior, our attitude and the culture we create. In the next section of this book you'll read quotes about the religious culture, mainly church as it has become.

What I said… "About Religious Culture

Authentic thoughts of Inspiration

What I said... "About Religious Culture"

- When we stop going to church just to say we went, and get back to having EXPERIENCES, perhaps people will begin to put the spiritual higher on the priority list. – *M L MARTIN*

- Eventually, we must get tired of spending all of our money running to conferences to hear the same thing your own Pastor said Sunday ...if you had just attended church. – *M L MARTIN*

- I'm not one of them people who go to church to just SIT in a room for an hour and a half.
  – *M L MARTIN*

- Christianity is not complicated.

  Everyone has Sinned. Everyone falls. Everyone has issues of some sort.

  But... Everyone won't repent.

  If you Sin, repent.

  If you fall, repent.

  It's not complicated. Just repent...

  If you repent, you'll be forgiven...

  Quit making excuses and provisions for the flesh... period. – *M L MARTIN*

- People want to just "have fun" until they die... because they know the preacher is going to lie for them at their funeral.

  Well, he can't lie for you at the great judgment.
  – *M L MARTIN*

- We're in a "put em out" generation...I'm from a "cast it out" generation… - *M L MARTIN*

- Wrong doesn't become right because YOU do it.
  – *M L MARTIN*

- Satan is not omniscient, omnipresent, or omnipotent. ...FYI - *M L MARTIN*

- It's extremely foolish to expect the sinner to live saved. – *M L MARTIN*

  You've got the Holy ghost and have trouble.
  – *M L MARTIN*

- I can argue either side of any argument...very well.

  I don't challenge your position, but how you arrived there. The pursuit is for truth & authenticity...not correctness of opinion.

...and THAT's how I study the word.
  – *M L MARTIN*

- Beating up people who have a different religion or denomination, seldomly (I repeat) VERY seldom proves to win people over. – *M L MARTIN*

- Ask me my "Denomination", I'm just going to tell you what I believe. – *M L MARTIN*

- Don't abuse your platform by pointlessly tearing people down...Use it to help lift people up.
  – *M L MARTIN*

- If for a second you have a thought that," this seems demonic." You're probably right. Be careful what you listen to, repeat, speak... power of life and death is in the tongue. – *M L MARTIN*

- Mario, why is everything so intense? Your prayer, your praise, your preaching....???

  Me: What I'm savin' it fuh? ("why would I save it?") – *M L MARTIN*

- We will break up over slow text messages.

  We will disown children if they never show up...

  Parents will keep kids away from baby daddy's that never call....

Yet WE say we love Jesus, and give him ZERO thoughts, and even look at folk crazy who dedicate time to "Love" him.

It's not what you say, it's what you DO, right?
– *M L MARTIN*

- The sermon ought not be designed to make you shout. It's supposed to be designed to make you BETTER. A fool hateth instruction, so they become angry about a sermon, while those that hunger and thirst after righteousness will rejoice on the word, even if it's a word of correction... You're not just rejoicing on the rebuke, you rejoice about freedom, because the TRUTH is what makes you free. That doesn't mean you're fake, it means you're grateful. – *M L MARTIN*

- The word of God is perfect. So many preachers are thirsty for oohs and ahhhs that they twist the word or leave it all together... The word doesn't need doctoring up, if they want oohs and ahhs send them to 6 flags. – *M L MARTIN*

When you're "trying" to sound deep, ...sometimes you sound dumb. – *M L MARTIN*

- You're never going to catch me apologizing for my religion, or spiritual beliefs... Ever. – *M L MARTIN*

- You can't have Gods word À la cart.
  – *M L MARTIN*

- Sometimes you experience church hurt and sometimes YOU hurt the Church. – *M L MARTIN*

- In every field, in every position, in every religion, denomination, genre, and/or profession you're going to find some people that have it all together, some still trying to get it/keep it together, and some completely satisfied without even having it together. Period. *– M L MARTIN*

- Uppity Christians had an attitude with Donnie McClurkin when "We fall down" came out... But, when their sins also came out, they seemed to have changed their attitude, on their way "back up".
  -M L MARTIN

- Stop trying to have Spiritual debates with the Carnal minded. *– M L MARTIN*

- We won't pray about them but we will often post about them. *– M L MARTIN*

- If you're tempted, Man... even if you gave in to temptation, you can start over. Don't let people shame you into continuing a sinful lifestyle! Thank God for Grace. *– M L MARTIN*

- The guy on TV may be a good preacher, but he will never be at you court date, hospital room, funeral... Don't forget to honor the lives of those who live for you! *– M L MARTIN*

- Stop shaming people for their struggles and lend them a hand! Consider your own difficulties, when you begin to put your mouth on others…
  – M L MARTIN

- Be not deceived... the DEVIL has ALWAYS been POLITE. *– M L MARTIN*

- I don't praise God because I got it all together... I praise God because I'm all messed up... Yet he STILL Loves me. #theRealWOKE – *M L MARTIN*

- I am convinced that some of the preachers that claim to be "called"... Must've been butt dialed by God. – *M L MARTIN*

- I wish more "Church leaders" would admit more frequently that they have faults... It'd be so much easier to explain to a non-believer if they didn't picture Christians as perfect people... Even the Biblical characters didn't have it together like many of you pretend to... – *M L MARTIN*

- Our society is facing a downward spiral, primarily because of the distortion of faith, disassembling of family, and disarray of morals. For, how can we decide WHO is right or wrong, if we are totally distracted from WHAT is right or wrong? life was meant to be peaceful, happy, and fun... But it must cease to be that momentarily in so much that the believer puts on fighting clothes, quit preparing for war and finally begin the fight... So, we may gain & maintain the Liberty to turn up. – *M L MARTIN*

- The church won't transform the community as long as its busy conforming to it... – *M L MARTIN*

Prayer WILL NOT WORK Just having a FORM of Godliness... Change will only occur when the people of God actually acknowledge God's Power in us! – *M L MARTIN*

- The goal of the Christian life isn't to get you to stop sinning, but rather to lead people to a lifestyle of love, laughter, abundance, and power. If we spend more time offering samples of Gods goodness and less time condemning people for our own individual interpretations of what sin is...THEN, and ONLY then will the Kingdom experience real growth, and your churches experience an overflow of souls.

~yep. I said it. – *M L MARTIN*

Self-reflection is one of the keys to a happier life. You'll never change what you do not notice or choose to ignore. Many are suffering from low self-worth, due to what they deem as lack of accomplishments. We must learn to hold ourselves accountable, encourage ourselves, and never give up. In this next section, you'll find some encouraging quotes, reminding you that you are capable beyond your imagination!

Quotes of Encouragement...

Authentic thoughts of Inspiration

Quotes of Encouragement...

Authentic thoughts of Inspiration

- I have NEVER QUIT in my life! I've moved on... but I DON'T Quit!
  – M L MARTIN

- KNOWING is half the battle… But DOING is the other, more difficult, most neglected half.
  – M L MARTIN

- You all can pretend if you want to...but it's a STRUGGLE trying to do EVERYTHING RIGHT at the same time!

  Live Right, Eat Right, and Exercise Right, manage Money Right, Be Positive...

  Don't believe all the Hype of people and their fake social media posts...

  Do the best you can, in every way you can, and strive to be BETTER... but, lift your head up and stop allowing yourself to be defeated by someone else's success... it's not a competition.

  – M L MARTIN

- Goals? Ok... Credit, summer body, Bae? All that's cool, but PLEASE Do Not undervalue the importance of a solid spiritual life.
  – M L MARTIN

- You actually MAY NOT be "Next in Line" for a miracle...But that doesn't mean you can't get your miracle NEXT! *– M L MARTIN*

- My character, my health, my self-esteem, my integrity, my zeal, my family, my finances, my vision... it's all been attacked...but, It's all still intact. *– M L MARTIN*

- Sometimes you need to think about all you've been through. Not for pity party purposes... but to remind yourself WHO and WHAT you are. Don't let your circumstances, failures, or lack make you forget about your DOPENESS.

  – M L MARTIN #encourageyourself.

- Ask ANY good basketball coach: When your shooter isn't hitting his shots, the answer is almost always "JUST KEEP SHOOTING". Living a saved life is not very different. I don't care how many times you miss the mark... JUST KEEP SHOOTING!

  – M L MARTIN

- They say to me, "You're ALWAYS doing something! Why don't you just REST awhile?!"

  I remind them that Thomas Edison said,

  "Restlessness is discontent and discontent is the first necessity of progress. Show me a thoroughly satisfied man and I will show you a failure."

  -So... I'll rest when I get the rest!
    – M L MARTIN

- It may not work out the way you thought.

  It might get worse before it gets better.

  ...but it WILL Work Out. ...it WILL Get Better.

  – M L MARTIN

- Here's the Truth. The World isn't getting any better. It is not going to. It's not supposed to. The Bible said perilous time we're coming... I guess, what I'm trying to say is that the World won't get better, ...but YOU CAN.

  – M L MARTIN

- I received confirmation that I can stop worrying about who doesn't understand me, and to not worry about what anyone thinks. I'm different. Different and dangerous. *– M L MARTIN*

- There's a word for people who constantly speak negativity about your goals and endeavors... They're called "who are you 's?". – *M L MARTIN*

- Listen:

  It doesn't matter WHAT they say... YOUR talent, gift, & abilities need not be in competition, nor does it need to meet the approval of anyone... esp. if you use it for God.

  Allow no one whom you think may have more experience, or maybe seen more... mitigate that anointing on your life.

  You better learn quickly to appreciate the uniqueness of your own abilities!

  My prayer today is that you seek to enhance your own talent and that God double stamp it with his approval and catapult you into a new dimension of blessings, pressed down, shaken together, and running over as a result of your obedient use of what he's given you! Receive it. – *M L MARTIN*

- Do you honestly think Mercedes Benz is even remotely concerned with how well Kia is doing?

  Nope. I don't. Because It's a different market, and a proven quality...

  When you are secure with yourself and the talents, capabilities, and potential in you...you don't have

time to be jealous, or afraid of another's progress...
But u can be like Mercedes and just continue in the
excellency of your greatness. -Selah

– M L MARTIN

- If You can take just a little more pain...

  God's going to give you a Lot more Power!

  – M L MARTIN

- "Don't let your emotions talk you out of your
  miracle." *– M L MARTIN*

  The question should never be "if you can?", ...but
  rather "HOW you will?".

  -M L MARTIN

- If you think your success is determined by people
  "liking" you...

  ...You're not ready.

  – M L MARTIN

- In a natural sense:

  I don't want to be perfect...I want to be me.

  – M L MARTIN

Being self-motivated is one sure fire way to succeed:

- **You don't base your efforts on your circumstances.**

- **You are always preparing for the next step.**

- **You never build your hopes and desires upon the opinions of others.**

It is important to try at all cost to remain hopeful.

In the next section, I share some quotes that will hopefully allow you to see that the same energy, and common sense that is applied to personal goals, can also be applied to relationship goals and situations. Read some of the quotes dealing with "Relationships"!

What I said…"About Dating"

Authentic thoughts of Inspiration

What I said…"About Dating"

Authentic thoughts of Inspiration

- I just want to tell all my Social Media Sisters... that "you don't HAVE to put on the red light! "There's a better way. – *M L MARTIN*

- I don't know about a summer body... but I'm here trying to get off SUMMER THIS FAT!
  – *M L MARTIN*

- You will end up happier looking for a RELATIONSHIP rather than a RELATIONS-ship? – *M L MARTIN*

- Bro, remember you find what you are looking for... gotta learn how to recognize "trouble" when you see it. – *M L MARTIN*

- One must learn how to be content alone... you can't keep a mate if you can't even keep yourself.
  – *M L MARTIN*

- It takes maturity to deal with reality... In ANY relationship, you must be mature enough to love people through phases and inevitable transitions... it's life. It's reality. People change. . Real, mature love remains the same.

  – *M L MARTIN*

■ The world has over sexualized everything. We have expanded, and exaggerated the sensual, and over emphasized the sexual nature of every being... so much so, that everything we see is through the lens of perversion...

On one hand, there are excessively conservative folk, that assume sex and sexual nature is the purest evil. Making up names for their children to call their "private parts", afraid to say the word SEX. Assume every woman that wears a form fitting, or wears even an elbow out are being lascivious... that alone pull out a breast to feed her baby. Preaching and churching has even been hindered because we act as if the ONLY sins are of a sexual nature. Dare we mention other sins and faults like gossip, conceit, or extended anger...Everything we see is SEX.

While on the other hand, there are those who feel like public nudity and showing, shaking, and sharing what your momma gave you to world is perfectly normal and sane... after all "it's YOUR body". Some ppl make every move, purchase, and discussion according to and based upon how "sexy" it will make him or her appear. Spending thousands of unnecessary dollars, to become sexier... Worshipping the body, the booty, and basking in the glory of beauty...here again, everything we see, is SEX.

If we would/could put less personal emphasis on "sex, and sexuality" (I said "personal emphasis") then our mindsets would change, certain acts

would never be committed, certain allegations
would never be made, and certain assumptions
about the mind of others would never be implied.
Yet, ...even this post, about excessively thinking
about sex...is about sex.
  – *M L MARTIN*

Some of Gods BEST and BLESSED gifts are
wrapped in some unique, peculiar, and
inexplicable packages... be careful what you leave
on the table just because you don't like the
wrapping paper.
  – *M L MARTIN*

- Many relationships are raggedy because people
  have adopted a new standard of selfishness in an
  attempt to abolish Gods original standard of
  selflessness. – *M L MARTIN*

- If they won't embrace your change for the better,
  they must become the change... for your better.
    – *M L MARTIN*

- EVERYTIME you go looking for something...
  you're going to find it. So, the question... what are
  you looking for? – *M L MARTIN*

- Ladies, spend less time dressing up your eyes, and
  more time working on your VISION.
    – *M L MARTIN*

- If they seem fake... ...they probably are.
    – *M L MARTIN*

- Sister why are you out here chasing drug dealers & getting pregnant… living off child support…Then, when he get shot and killed you don't have any Social Security to help you because he never had a job.

  – M L MARTIN

- Brothers are ignoring chicks that can throw in the kitchen for a bad b**** that can't even separate an Oreo...*– M L MARTIN*

- God said be fruitful AND multiply... They are NOT the same thing... Everybody out here multiplying yet they still aren't producing any fruit.... Therefore, we now have a world filled with nothingness.... That's why you can't link up with everyone.. Nothing from Nothing leaves NOTHING! *– M L MARTIN*

- If you don't appreciate what you've got... And you can't celebrate who you've got... You will definitely lose them. #relationships

  – M L MARTIN

- Some guys will cheat on his new chick with his ex-chick using the same excuse he gave the new chick for cheating on his ex-chick. *– M L MARTIN*

- A lot of people learned you need to be SURE when you link up or get married, but it's equally as important to be SURE that when you Break up or Divorce, that the love is gone... basically, stop

making heart decisions, based on convenience
  – *M L MARTIN*

- Wives: don't be weary in well doing... it looks like the Hoes are winning... they're not. -Don't cross over, they need an example. – *M L MARTIN*

- Sometimes YOU are the problem in SOMEONE ELSES life...quit trying to find someone to blame and get yourself together. – *M L MARTIN*

- "Be yourself is not always sound advice, because most people don't even know who that is."
  – *M L MARTIN*

- The saying goes: "Love is not what you say, it's what you Do!"

  I'd say, "Love is not just what you DO... it's HOW you do!"

  – *M L MARTIN*

- Don't let those late-night thoughts creep into your early-morning actions.
  – *M L MARTIN*

- Husbands/Wives:

  Stop being so quick to pray that God "fix" your spouse, but rather, pray he reveal how to fix YOUR flesh, and alter YOUR attitude in a way that's pleasing to HIM, and enhancing to your marriage.   – *M L MARTIN*

Show me someone who won't admit what they did... and nine times out of ten I'll be looking at someone who's still doing it.

– M L MARTIN

- I can tell how mature you are by what you think is attractive.
  – M L MARTIN

To have or maintain a healthy relationship, I must first be willing to relate...

In the next section you will read several quotes and thoughts I have regarding social subjects and relationships. These quotes may or may not get under your skin. I don't intend to offend anyone. I am also not expecting everyone to agree. My hope is that you will at least consider some of the thoughts that these quotes may provoke.

Social Quotes

Authentic thoughts of Inspiration

Social Quotes

- It's frustrating to hear people who aren't black ask, "Why can they say it (n word), and we can't?"...

  First of all, ...You're meddling.
  – M L MARTIN

- Parents,

  In your pursuit of a new life, New level, and new locations, etc... Don't leave behind or neglect your most important luggage...those kids will one day want to be successful too... Don't just do it FOR them, do it WITH them, so they can know how.

  – M L MARTIN

- Stop" trying" to go through it alone... If you don't have to. I know it's hard to trust people with your feelings, but a friend that will listen and not judge you are a huge blessing. *– M L MARTIN*

- Black people should not complain about black businesses until they become better black customers to black business.
  – M L MARTIN

- It's funny to me how folk are frequently, "Cancelling" people you've never supported in the first place!

  – M L MARTIN

- The suffering of our generation is the result of unparented parents.

  – M L MARTIN

- Black people aren't OVERLY SENSITIVE... Compare our reactions to subtle racism to the way a woman reacts to "playful Love taps"... after her husband has beaten her for nearly 400 years...

  – M L MARTIN

- When a preacher's whole sermon is about another preacher... he isn't preaching.

  – M L MARTIN

- I'm often incredibly frustrated with those in the black community that will idolize Drug dealers, murderers, and well-known people because of this stupid standard of what it means to be cool. Yet, ridicule and have hatred for good people that want us to do better, be better, and be accountable for ourselves. *– M L MARTIN*

- Everyone's fighting for CIVIL RIGHTS...Is there anyone fighting for LIVING RIGHT? – *M L MARTIN*

- It's called government "assistance". Not government "do it for me". – *M L MARTIN*

- . Do you wonder why Jail seldomly works? Because Jail has no power.

  You think he's a Killer just because he's a gangster...

  You think he's a Murderer just because he's Poor....

  I'm telling you he's a got a Demon.

  Most of these murders are simply the manifestation of demonic presence and influence.

  They don't need the electric chair, they need the Holy ghost.

  – M L MARTIN

Not much to summarize here. I said it. I meant it. I'm not taking it back.

The next section contains random proverbial statements. Many of these are thought provoking. Although a hint of sarcasm may be detected, they were really intended to produce positive behavioral adjustments.

Random Proverbial Quotes

Authentic thoughts of Inspiration

Random Proverbial Quotes

- A complaint without even attempting a solution is a contribution to the problem.
  – M L MARTIN

- Being an Adult has nothing to do with the size of your jeans and jewelry... if you want Adult respect, you're going to have to act as an Adult. *– M L MARTIN*

- It's easy to criticize what you have NEVER had to do. *– M L MARTIN*

- Period. Plain and simple. People sow into what & who they believe in. No argument about it. *– M L MARTIN*

- When you're really trying to help ppl, you don't have to worry about being appreciated... Keep doing good, you never know who's watching!

  – M L MARTIN

- I'm saddened by the number of people holding on to grudges and unforgiveness in their hearts for things they were meddling about in the first place… *– M L MARTIN*

- Judge people by patterns, not incidents.
  – M L MARTIN

- Only a liar won't call a liar a liar.
  – M L MARTIN

- Don't be fooled by online experts who haven't accomplished anything…👀 How can you have SO MANY answers, but never passed a TEST? *– M L MARTIN*

- Don't hate on styles you don't like. Instead, learn to appreciate the styles, and artistic nature of others. This is for Singers, Rappers, Preachers, Ball Players, Actors, DJ's, Parents, Bill collectors, salesmen, I mean literally everyone. We are all made different, so why would we all express ourselves the same?

  – M L MARTIN

- A true sign of maturity is learning not to respond to everything said, every lie told, every blatantly inappropriate remark, unappreciative action, or unnecessary attack. – *M L MARTIN*

- Love. Pray. Forgive. Ask for Forgiveness. Repeat. – *M L MARTIN*

- You can be doing the right thing, yet still have consequences for when you didn't.
  – *M L MARTIN*

- We glorify the causer of our pain yet neglect to acknowledge the person MOST responsible for our healing. At some point YOU have to assume the responsibility of initiating a spiritual wellness.
  –*M L MARTIN*

- Stop expecting "people" to be perfect. This will help YOU when handling other people's faults, while simultaneously helping YOU accept the criticisms that we SO OFTEN need, yet won't always come across perfectly. For, how can an imperfect person expect imperfect people to address imperfections, perfectly? – *M L MARTIN*

- Tantrums don't scare troubles away.
  – *M L MARTIN*

- Try to make sure your attitude, energy, and skill match each other.
  – *M L MARTIN*

- You can't resolve an internal problem with external restrictions…
  – M L MARTIN

- There's a fine line between being "professional" and being "extra".
  – M L MARTIN

- Often, it's the most flawed people that tend to do the most shaming?
  – M L MARTIN

- There are a lot of things to be concerned about:

  •Killers on the loose...

  •Innocent victims everywhere...

  •we are in a state of emergency...

  •YOU could be next...

  ....and your only concerns are Tittie Tuesday and how the weed smells?

  – M L MARTIN

- One can know ALL the inspirational quotes, scriptures, songs, and scenarios... Yet still feel discouraged, down, and defeated *– M L MARTIN*

- One should spend more time completing their resume than their Tattoo…

   – M L MARTIN

- I just want people to be happy and go to heaven. ...and shut up.   (not in that order)

   – M L MARTIN

- If you can't support me at KFC.. Don't sweat me at the YUM ctr.

   – M L MARTIN

- Character drives Talent toward Greatness... And Talent with an absence of Character will birth creative ways to produce perpetual laziness.

   – M L MARTIN

- Confidence is good. Over confidence begets cockiness, and cockiness begets, lack of support. First, you need to acknowledge that your project may not be everything you meant it to be. Acknowledge that you aren't everything yet that you aim to be... Then, humbly solicit support. Nothing is worse than someone who is possibly talented (and I say possibly because just because you think it doesn't necessarily mean you are) acting as if we OWE you support because you are the greatest. Many of you act like you are already there, you already made it, if that's so... You don't need us anyway. Stop getting upset because nobody wanted to buy your project... Do research, learn your customers, learn your fan base, and most importantly... Expect and accept honest criticism of your talents, and stop listening to your "DO-boys"! You call a hater anyone that tells you that you can do better, but call your friends "supporters" when they tell you that bathroom sounding studio track is the next big thing... It's not, and they aren't supporting you, they are lying to you.

- "The devil wants to distract you with your problem, so you won't use your Power".   – M L MARTIN

- The real test of character is in your ability to "love" those that don't even "like" you...   – M L MARTIN

- Don't allow the "moment" you're in make a mockery of you. You're better than going off, giving up, or stooping to someone else's level...You have more character than that... Overcome your moments of weakness, and convert them

into winning testimonies!
– M L MARTIN

* You find what you're looking for. You get what you expect...I see and feel positive energy, because that's all I give credit too! Learn to shake off the negativity and choose NOT to complain!

– M L MARTIN

* You can't be yourself until you know yourself, quit making long term decisions based on temporary happiness... it's ok to be patient.

– M L MARTIN

* **SMAR•PID -**

  1. The act of being so smart, you're stupid.

  2. The state of having an abundance of knowledge yet overlooking key basic and common sense facts.

  3. The unnecessary use of words, quotes, formulas and/or theories to evaluate and come to obvious conclusions.

  ...Don't be **smarpid**.
– M L MARTIN

- Your circle may disqualify you from certain connections.

  – M L MARTIN

- "Pride goeth before destruction, and a haughty spirit before a fall" Proverbs 16:18

  Ask for help. Quit down talking people. Treat people with dignity and respect. Don't put others down to puff yourself up. Learn when to shut up. *– M L MARTIN*

- The only plausible requests for support should come from the folks who have actually proven themselves supportive.

  I can't stand someone who only:

  1. stands when it's their turn to sing

  2. laughs at their own jokes

  3. Amens their own statements

  4. pats themselves on the back

  ...then expects everyone else throw rose pedals.

Be not deceived, God is not mocked...

whatsoever a man soweth, THAT shall he also reap...
> — *M L MARTIN*

- If you spent more time praying for the people your running your mouth about... the world, their life, and YOURS would be SO MUCH BETTER!
  > — *M L MARTIN*

- Maturity is admitting how messed up you used to be, and not being afraid to talk about it.   — *M L MARTIN*

- When the work got hard, I asked God to send me "some" help...then God said, "keep working I'm about to send you "to" help".

> — *M L MARTIN*

- Be not deceived... God is not mocked. For "WHAT-SO-EVER" a man soweth, "THAT" shall he also reap.

What -EVER kind of seed you plant will grow.

SO:

•Instead of discord - sow peace

•Instead of anger - sow laughter

•Instead of teaching kids that Jordan's and valuables are most important, teach them to GIVE and care for the poor.

•Instead of giving celebrity relationships so much attention, pay attention to your OWN lover.

•Instead of watching Love & Hip Hop - read something positive.

...then wait.

The next section is the section that I value the most. It has become my personal calling as a Pastor and certified Life Coach to aide as many others as possible in the effort of making and meeting an appointment with their purpose. My prayer is that upon reading these quotes, you will find one that sticks with you, or that many will inspire you and that you will be propelled into a higher cycle of achievement.

What I said about "Purpose"

Authentic thoughts of Inspiration

What I said about "Purpose"

- Pride can be an enemy of Progress...
  Your Goals aren't serious until you're willing to allow your Grind to disrespect your Pride.

  — M L MARTIN

- "It's impossible to Live beyond Limits if you do not Live beyond Labels."
  — M L MARTIN

- The longevity of my dopeness derives from my ability to understand one thing. That is that my productivity isn't predicated on anyone's opinion of me...

  — M L MARTIN

- Hold very little value in the opinionated criticisms of people who don't know what they're talking about.
  — M L MARTIN

- You must understand your value... even when others don't!
    – M L MARTIN

- Don't live your life trying to reach goals that other people have set for you. Those that like you will often fail to push you to reach high enough, while those that hate will always keep moving the goal out of your reach.
    – M L MARTIN

- Just because they're not what you are, doesn't mean there's something wrong with you.   *– M L MARTIN*

- The Validation of my Destiny is not Predicated on your Presumption...
    – M L MARTIN

- Even Drug Dealers need to know the times table.
    – M L MARTIN

- When you pray for rain, you must be willing to deal with the mud.

    -M L MARTIN

- The next level of purpose requires that you acknowledge the enemy driving your enemies... Remember, we wrestle with spirits, not people... and you can't CAST OUT, what you won't CALL OUT.

  – M L MARTIN

- They won't give you the benefit of doubt, because they don't like you...

  -M L MARTIN

- When Change is calling...You're going to have to click answer or ignore?

  – M L MARTIN

- They want you to stay in your lane, but you have been CHOSEN to pave the way!

  -M L MARTIN

One thing regarding purpose is that while we were all created for a purpose, the purpose doesn't belong to us. The purpose belongs to God. The day you find out what that purpose is, is a day that you will never forget!

Thank you for reading my quotes!

Please share with a friend!